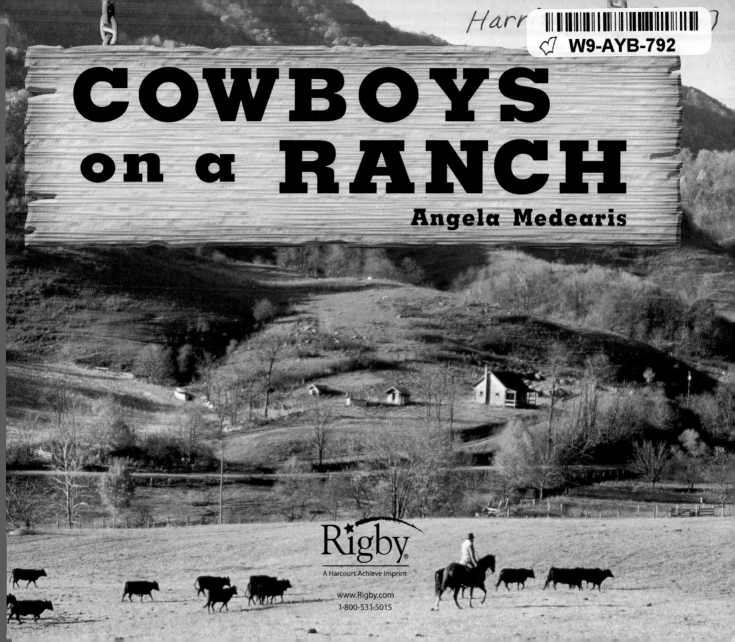

COWBOYS on a RANCH

Angela Medearis

Rigby®
A Harcourt Achieve Imprint

www.Rigby.com
1-800-531-5015

A cowboy has a very busy life.

The work on a ranch begins
early in the morning.

Cowboys wake up and put on jeans,
hats, and boots.
Some of them wear chaps over their jeans.
Sometimes cowboys go into thick bushes.
Chaps keep a cowboy's legs
from getting thorns on them.
Mexican cowboys made
the first chaps.

Cowboys also wear cowboy hats.

These hats keep cowboys cool.

Hats keep their heads dry in the rain, too.

Some cowboys use their hats to give
the horses food and water.

Cowboys work very hard on a ranch.

They have a lot of jobs to do.

The cowboys fix all the fences on the ranch.

The fences keep the cattle
from running away.

Cowboys take care of the cattle.
They count the cattle and put special tags on their ears.
The tags have numbers on them to help the cowboys keep track of the cattle.

Cowboys feed the cattle and give them water.
Cowboys take the cattle out to the field.
Exercise and fresh grass are good
for the cattle.
Cowboys make sure the cattle are healthy.

Now the work on the ranch is done
for the day.

The fences are fixed, and the cattle are safe.

The cowboys are hungry.

It's dinnertime!

Index